SECRET CODES 2
for
Nintendo
64®

STRATEGY GUIDES

LEGAL STUFF

Secret Codes 2 for Nintendo 64®

Brady Publishing
An Imprint of
Macmillan Digital Publishing USA
201 W. 103rd Street
Indianapolis, Indiana 46290

ISBN: 1-56686-798-3

Library of Congress Catalog No.: 97-070266

Printing Code: The rightmost double-digit number is the year of the book's printing; the rightmost single-digit number is the number of the book's printing. For example, 98-1 indicates that the first printing of the book occurred in 1998.
01 00 99 98   4 3 2

Manufactured in the United States of America.

Duke Nukem 64 Duke Nukem is a trademark of 3D Realms Entertainment. Duke Nukem ©1997 3D Realms Entertainment.

FIFA: Road to World Cup '98 ©1997 Electronic Arts. All Rights Reserved.

Fighter's Destiny™ is a trademark of Imagineer. ©1997 Imagineer.

Forsaken™ & ©1997 Acclaim Entertainment, Inc. All rights reserved.

Goldeneye 007™ ©1997 Nintendo/Rare. ©1962, 1995 Danjaq, LLC & UAC. All rights reserved. ©1997 Eon Productions Ltd. & Mac B. Inc.

Kobe Bryant in NBA Courtside ©1998 NBA Properties, Inc. All rights reserved. ©1998 Nintendo.

Mace: The Dark Age ©1997 Atari Games Corp. All rights reserved. Midway is a registered trademark of Midway Games Inc.

Madden Football 64 Software ©1997 Electronic Arts. John Madden Football is a trademark of Electronic Arts. All rights reserved.

Major League Baseball® Featuring Ken Griffey Jr. ©1998 Nintendo of America Inc. ©MLBPA. Official Licensee—Major League Baseball Players Association.

Mortal Kombat Mythologies: Sub-Zero Mortal Kombat® Mythologies™: Sub-Zero ©1997 Midway Games Inc. All rights reserved. MORTAL KOMBAT, the DRAGON DESIGN, SUB-ZERO and all other character names are trademarks of Midway Games Inc.

BradyGAMES Staff

Publisher
Lynn Zingraf

Editor-In-Chief
H. Leigh Davis

Title/Licensing Manager
David Waybright

Marketing Manager
Janet Cadoff

Acquisitions Editor
Debra McBride

Credits

Project Editors
David Bartley
Tim Cox

Screenshot Editor
Michael Owen

Creative Director/Book Designer
Scott Watanabe

Production Designer
Dan Caparo
Dave Eason
Jane Washburne

CONTENTS

A Note About the GameShark Codes

PLEASE READ THE FOLLOWING!

It's extremely important that you take note of the following information concerning the GameShark codes in this book. So, before you write us a letter saying that a GameShark code doesn't work, take a few minutes to read what follows.

Different Versions of GameShark

There are many different versions of the GameShark on the market. We have the N64 GameShark Version 2.0, which is what we used to check the codes in this book. Therefore, if you're using a different version of the GameShark, some of the codes may not work on your game.

Key Code

A few games require a Key Code, such as Diddy Kong Racing, 1080 Snowboarding, and Yoshi's Story. You must have at least Version 1.08 of the GameShark. Keep in mind that since we are using Version 2.0, our Key Codes may not work with other versions.

GS Button

The GS Button is located to the right of the LED display on the front of the GameShark. When pressed while using a certain code, the GS button increases the number of items on-screen or it may even turn on a code. The GS button can be used on almost any game.

CODES LEGEND

Abbreviation:	What It Means:
A	A button
B	B button
C-Up	Top C button
C-Right	Right C button
C-Down	Bottom C button
C-Left	Left C button
Right	Right on D-pad
Down	Down on D-pad
Left	Left on D-pad
Up	Up on D-pad
L Shift	Left Shoulder button on top
R Shift	Right Shoulder button on top

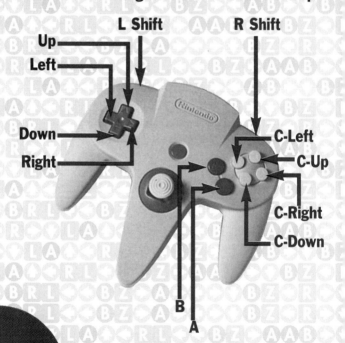

10

1080 SNOWBOARDING

Penguin Board

Perform all 24 tricks in training Training Mode, then when you select your board hold C-Down while you select the Tahoe 151.

Easy Tricks in Training Mode

To perform the more difficult tricks in Training Mode, perform an easy trick and then quickly press C-Right to access the trick menu. Then change the move you just executed to a more difficult move. Now when you land, it should give you credit for the tougher trick.

Dragon Cave Course

In Match Race, reach the fifth course on Hard difficulty.

Deadly Fall Course

In Match Race, reach the sixth course on Expert difficulty.

Panda Boarder

Get the high score/best time in all the Time Attacks and Trick Attacks. Then get all three best scores in the Contest Mode. Then at the player select screen, highlight Rob Haywood and confirm your choice by holding C-Right and pressing A.

Crystal Boarder

Defeat the expert level in Match Race. Then at the player select screen, highlight Akari Hayami and confirm your choice by holding C-Left and pressing A.

Golden Boarder

Defeat the expert level in Match Race using the Crystal Boarder. Then at the player select screen, highlight Kensuke Kimachi and confirm your choice by holding C-Up and pressing A.

GameShark Codes

These codes require an N64 Keycode GameShark.

EFFECT	CODE
Keycode	50F249087C07EE6C25
Enable Codes	DE0004000000
Match Levels Completed	8025508A0005
Enable All Levels	8125508800FF
Infinite Lives	8026B1CB0003

AEROFIGHTERS ASSAULT

Stage Select

During the intro scenes enter the following code: Up, C-Down, Left, C-Right, Down, C-Up, Right, C-Left, L Shift, R-Shift, Z. You should hear a chime if the code worked.

Enable Mao Mao

At the Title screen press C-Left, C-Down, C-Right, C-Up, C-Left, C-Right, C-Down. At the Plane Select screen, you should see a new F-15 with a new pilot.

Hidden Pilot

To get Spanky, the second hidden pilot, you must find and complete all the bonus stages in the game.

Change Aircraft Colors

When selecting an aircraft in the Main Game, Boss Attack or Practice Modes, press Left/Right on the joy-stick to select an aircraft. Press R Shift to toggle between an aircraft's color schemes. Press A or Start to confirm your selection.

GameShark Codes

EFFECT	CODE
Extra Planes	8127CCECFFFF
Infinite Chaffs	8027E017000A
Infinite Special Weapons	8027E4D20002

AERO GAUGE

All Tracks and All Vehicles

Turn on the game and press Start on controller 1 until the "Push Start" screen appears. Then on controller 2, press Up, C-Down, R Shift, L Shift, and Z at the same time, and then release them. Press Start or the A button on controller 1 to enter the Grand Prix mode. You should now have access to all the tracks and vehicles in all modes.

China Town Jam Track

To access the China Town Jam Track, you must race in Grand Prix mode with the difficulty level set to Expert. Defeat the game with a first place ranking on each course to gain access to the new track.

Drive the N64 Controller

To drive as an N64 controller, choose the Time Attack Mode. If you get a race time that ends in point zero six four seconds (.064), the controller will become available.

Get the Dominator

To gain the Dominator aeromachine, you must finish the game in first place on Expert difficulty level using the Black Lighting.

Get the Prowler

To gain the Prowler aeromachine, you must finish the game in first place on Expert difficulty level using the Hornet car.

Get the Reaper

To gain the Reaper aeromachine, you must finish the game in first place on Expert difficulty level using the Shredder car.

REAPER

Get the Vengeance

To gain the Vengeance aeromachine, you must finish the game in first place on Expert difficulty level using the Avenger.

Neo Speed Way Track

To get the Neo Speed Way Track, you must race in Grand Prix mode with the difficulty level set to Intermediate. Defeat the game with a first place ranking on each course to access the new track.

NEO SPEED WAY

Turbo Boost
Press and hold the A button during the race and drift hard to the left or right by holding the Z trigger. Release both buttons to get the boost.

ALL-STAR BASEBALL '99

Big Heads and Feet
Enter BIGHELIUM in the Cheat Menu to get big heads and feet.

Big Head, Big Bat, Big Feet Mode
Enter GOTHELIUM in the Cheat Menu to get big heads.

Paper-thin Players
Enter PRPPAPLYR in the Cheat Menu to get extremely thin players.

AUTOMOBILI LAMBORGHINI

Bonus Cars
You earn new cars for each series you defeat.

EASY

Arcade: Basic Series - Porsche 959
Arcade: Pro Series – Ferrari 512 TR
Normal Championship Series –
Bugatti EB110 GT

EXPERT

Arcade: Basic Series – Ferrari F-50
Arcade: Pro Series – Dodge Viper GTS
Normal Championship Series –
McLaren F1 and reverse tracks are
opened

Reverse Tracks

Defeat the Championship Mode in Novice and Expert difficulty levels.

GameShark Codes

EFFECT	CODE
100 Points	800CE7430064
Infinite Time	800CE76F0063
Extra Vehicles	800985C30001
	800985C50001
	800985C70001
	800985CB0001
	800985CD0001
	800985CF0001

BIO FREAKS

First Person Cam

This cheat can only be enabled during a 1-player game. At the same time, press Back on the D-pad and the Start button. You can return to the default

camera mode by pressing Back (which is now Down on the D-pad) and Start.

Mutilations

Fighter	Move
BullzEye	→, ←, RP
Delta	→, ← + LK
Minatek	← + LP + LK
PsyClown	→, ← + LP + LK
Purge	←, → + RP + RK
Sabotage	←, ←, RP + RK
Ssapo	→, ← + RP + RK
ZipperHead	→, ← + RP

BLAST CORPS

GameShark Codes

EFFECT	CODE
Infinite Hydraulics Sidesweeper	803EDB510063
Infinite Missiles Motor Bike	803F8AC30063

BOMBERMAN 64

Bonus World
Collect all 100 Gold Cards and defeat Altair again to access Rainbow Palace.

View Credits
Defeat the game with 100 Gold Cards, and then finish the extra world by

A B C D E F G H I J K L M N O P Q R S T U V W X Y Z

defeating Sirius. A new view credits option should appear at the Options menu.

Sound Test

Defeat the game in Adventure Mode on Normal difficulty.

Bonus Battle Levels

At the Main menu, press Start repeatedly until you hear a chime.

GameShark Codes

EFFECT	CODE
Battle Mode "Blizzard Battle" Stage	802AC61F0008 802AC7030008
Battle Mode "In The Gutter" Stage	802AC61F0006 802AC7030006

Battle Mode	802AC61F0009
"Lost At Sea"	802AC7030009
Stage	
Battle Mode	802AC61F0007
"Sea Sick" Stage	802AC7030007

EFFECT	CODE
Gems	802AC62f0063
Infinite Credits	802AC62B0063
Infinite Lives	802AC6270063
Stop Timer	802AC6430000

BUST-A-MOVE 2: ARCADE EDITION

Another World

At the Title screen, press L Shift, Up, R Shift, and Down. When entered correctly, a little green character should appear in the corner of the Title screen. There should be a new "Another World" option in Puzzle Mode.

GameShark Codes

EFFECT	CODE
Infinite Credits	801201710005

CHAMELEON TWIST

Bonus Level

Collect all the crowns and defeat the Boss to access the Bonus Level.

Play Pool

In Stage 6, the Ghost Castle, instead of going upstairs in the first room, go to the locked door near the rabbit. If you have at least 50 crowns, you will be allowed in to play a game of pool.

GameShark Codes

EFFECT	CODE
Access All Levels	8020850E00FF
	8020851000FF
Extra Crowns	802517670015

CLAY FIGHTER 63 ⅓

Hidden Fighters

To access the hidden fighters, enter the following at the Character Select screen:

CHARACTER	CODE
Dr. Kiln	Hold L Shift and press B, C-Left, C-Up, C-Right, C-Down, A
Sumo Santa	Hold L Shift and press A, C-Down, C-Right, C-Up, C-Left, B
Boogerman	Hold L Shift and press Up, Right, Down, Left, Right, Left

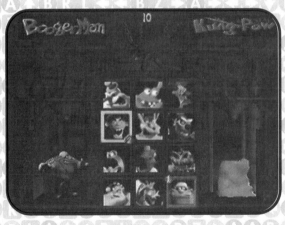

Secret Options Menu

At the Character Select screen, hold L Shift and press C-Up, C-Right, C-Left, C-Down, B, A.

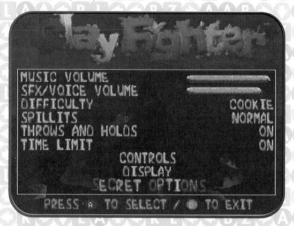

```
MUSIC VOLUME
SFX/VOICE VOLUME
DIFFICULTY                        COOKIE
SPILLITS                          NORMAL
THROWS AND HOLDS                      ON
TIME LIMIT                            ON
              CONTROLS
              DISPLAY
           SECRET OPTIONS
   PRESS A TO SELECT / ● TO EXIT
```

```
CHOOSE BACKGROUND (1 PLAYER)          ON
BODY TYPE                        MASSIVE
VOICE                               HIGH
CAMERA FLIGHTS                        ON
CLAYTALITY TIMER                     OFF
MOVE CAMERA WITH FOURTH PAD          OFF

        PRESS ♦ OR ● TO EXIT
```

Stage Select

When the Versus Screen appears in 2-player mode, press C-Right or C-Left to select a different stage.

IN
KILN'S LABORATORY

Random Select

To randomly select a character, hold
L Shift + R Shift at the Character
Select screen.

GameShark Codes

EFFECT	CODE
Extra Characters/ Secret Options	801A2B41000F

CLAYFIGHTER 63 ⅓ SCULPTOR'S CUT

Play as Sumo Santa

At the Character Select screen, hold Z
or L Shift and press A, C-Right, A,
C-Right, C-Down, C-Up. You should
hear a sound when entered correctly.
To access Sumo Santa, press R Shift
while on the question mark.

Play as Boogerman

At the Character Select screen, hold Z or L Shift and press B, B, C-Right, C-Right, C-Left, C-Right. You should hear a sound when entered correctly. To access Boogerman, press R Shift while on the question mark.

Play as High Five

At the Character Select screen, hold Z or L Shift and press C-Up, C-Down, C-Left, C-Right, B, A. You should hear a sound when entered correctly. To play as High Five, press R Shift while on the question mark.

Play as Earthworm Jim

At the Character Select screen, hold Z or L Shift and press B, C-Left , C-Up , C-Right , C-Down , C-Up. You should hear a sound when entered correctly. To play as Earthworm Jim, press R Shift while on the question mark.

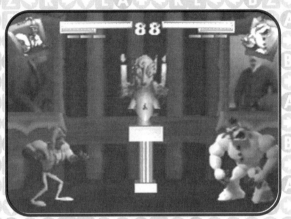

Random Select

To randomly select a character, hold L Shift + R Shift at the Character Select screen or select one of the question mark squares.

Change Color

To change colors, press C-Down instead of A when selecting your character.

A B C D E F G H I J K L M N O P Q R S T U V W X Y Z

DARK RIFT

Boss Codes

To access the Bosses in Dark Rift, you must enter the following codes at the Title screen:

Boss	Press
Sonork	Left, Right, C-Up, C-Down, C-Left, C-Right
Demitron and Sonork	A, B, Right, Left, C-Down, C-Up

Character Endings

To access each character's ending, you must enter the following codes at the Title screen:

Character	Press
Aaron	Up, C-Left, R Shift, Right, Down, R Shift, R Shift, C-Left
Demonica	Up, C-Left, R Shift, Right, Down, R Shift, R Shift, C-Up

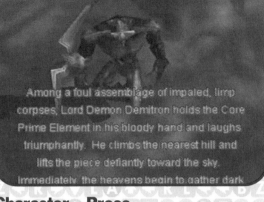

Among a foul assemblage of impaled, limp
corpses, Lord Demon Demitron holds the Core
Prime Element in his bloody hand and laughs
triumphantly. He climbs the nearest hill and
lifts the piece defiantly toward the sky.
Immediately, the heavens begin to gather dark

Character	Press
Demitron	Up, C-Left, R Shift, Right, Down, L Shift, L Shift, C-Down
Eve	Up, C-Left, R Shift, Right, Down, R Shift, R Shift, C-Right
Gore	Up, C-Left, R Shift, Right, Down, R Shift, R Shift, C-Down
Morphix	Up, C-Left, R Shift, Right, Down, R Shift, R Shift, B
Niiki	Up, C-Left, R Shift, Right, Down, R Shift, R Shift, A
Scarlet	Up, C-Left, R Shift, Right, Down, L Shift, L Shift, C-Left
Sonork	Up, C-Left, R Shift, Right, Down, L Shift, L Shift, C-Up
Zenmuron	Up, C-Left, R Shift, Right, Down, L Shift, L Shift, C-Right

GameShark Codes

EFFECT	CODE
Enable Demitron	80049DF40001
Enable Sonork	80049DF00001

DIDDY KONG RACING

Cheat Codes

You must enter the following codes at the Enter Cheat screen. You can turn the codes on and off by accessing the Enter Cheat screen.

MAGIC CODES LIST

HORN CHEAT	ON
DISABLE WEAPONS	OFF
DISABLE BANANAS	OFF
BANANAS REDUCE SPEED	OFF
NO LIMIT TO BANANAS	OFF
ALL BALLOONS ARE RED	OFF
ALL BALLOONS ARE GREEN	OFF
ALL BALLOONS ARE YELLOW	OFF
ALL BALLOONS ARE RAINBOW	OFF
TWO PLAYER ADVENTURE	OFF

Code	Effect
WHODIDTHIS	View the game credits
FREEFRUIT	Start with 10 bananas
TOXICOFFENDER	All balloons are green
DOUBLEVISION	Two players can use the same character
OPPOSITESATTRACT	All balloons are rainbows
BODYARMOR	All balloons are yellow
BOMBSAWAY	All balloons are red
ROCKETFUEL	All balloons are blue

NOYELLOWSTUFF	No bananas in multi-player mode
BYEBYEBALLOONS	Computer can't use weapons
JOINTVENTURE	Two-player Adventure

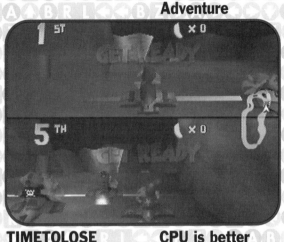

TIMETOLOSE	CPU is better
BLABBERMOUTH	Changes horn sounds
BOGUSBANANAS	Bananas slow you down
VITAMINB	Unlimited bananas
ZAPTHEZIPPERS	No zippers
FREEFORALL	Fully powered-up balloons
JUKEBOX	Adds Music Test to Audio Options Menu
ARNOLD	Large players
TEENYWEENIES	Small players
OFFROAD	4-wheel drive

Play as TT

Defeat TT's record time in all 20 courses with the selected vehicle in Time Challenge. TT should appear on the Character Select screen.

Play as Drumstick

After collecting all of the amulets, go to the main area. Find the frog with the red "hair piece" and run over it.

GameShark Codes

This game requires a Keycode GameShark.

EFFECT	CODE
Keycode	50F249087C07EE6C25
Enable Codes	DE0004000000
50 Balloons	801FCBED0032
Cheat Menu for Tracks Mode	810DFD9EFFFF

DOOM 64

GameShark Codes

EFFECT	CODE
Always Have BFG 9000	800632DB0001
Always Have Chain Gun	800632CF0001
Always Have Missile Launcher	800632D30001
Always Have Plasma Rifle	800632D70001
Gun/Chain Gun Ammo	800632E300ff
Invincibility	8006330B0002
Missile Ammo	800632EF0064
Plasma/BFG/Weapons Ammo	800632EB0064
Always Have Chainsaw	800632BB0001
Always Have Double Shotgun	800632CB0001
Always Have Gun	800632C30001
Always Have Shotgun	800632C70001
Blue Key	8006328f0001
Blue Skull Key	8006329B0001
Red Key	800632970001
Red Skull Key	800632A30001
Shotgun Ammo	800632E70064
Yellow Key	800632930001
Yellow Skull Key	8006329F0001

DUKE NUKEM 64

Cheat Menu

At the Main menu, press Left, Left, L Shift, L Shift, Right, Right, Left, Left. This opens up a Cheat Menu.

No Monsters

This code enables you to turn the monsters off or on in the Levels. To enter this code, first enter the Cheat Menu code. While still at the Title screen, press L Shift, C-Left, Left, R Shift, C-Right, Right, Left, Left.

Level Skip

At the Title screen, enter the code for the Cheat Menu. While still at the Title screen, press L Shift (x3), C-Right, Right, Left, Left, C-Left.

All Items

Enter the Cheat Menu code as shown previously, then return to the Main menu and press R Shift, C-Right, Right, L Shift, C-Left, Left, C-Right, Right.

Invincibility

Enter the Cheat Menu code as shown previously, then press R Shift (X7) and then Left. When entered correctly, you'll hear a tone. You can turn on the Invincibility option in the Cheat Menu.

Dancing Duke

In Cooperative or Dukematch Mode, shoot another Duke with the Expander and pause the game before he explodes. Then access the Cheat Menu and turn on Invincibility. Return to the game and access the Cheat Menu again to turn off Invincibility.

Little Duke

In Cooperative or Dukematch Mode, shoot another Duke with the Shrinker and then access the Cheat Menu and turn on and off Invincibility. Doing this causes the affected Duke to remain small for the rest of the game or until he gets stepped on.

Big Duke

In Cooperative or Dukematch Mode, shoot another Duke with the Expander, let him grow, and then pause the game before he explodes. Access the Cheat Menu and turn on and off Invincibility. Return to the game and that Duke should be an easy target.

GameShark Codes

EFFECT	CODE
Infinite Grenades	802A5A0700FF
Infinite Jet Pack	812A5A8E0640
Grenade Launcher	812A5ABC0101
Cheat Menu	801012D80001
	801012DC0001
	801012E00001
	801012E40001
	801012E80001
Expander/Missile Launcher	812A5AC00101
Have All Keys	802A5A47000F
Infinite Expander Ammo	802A5A0D00FF
Infinite Laser Trip Bomb Ammo	802A5A1300FF
Infinite Missiles	802A5A0F00FF
Infinite Pipe Bomb Ammo	802A5A0900FF
Infinite Plasma Ammo	802A5A1100FF
Infinite Shrinker Ammo	802A5A0B00FF
Pipe Bombs/Shrinker	812A5ABE0101
Plasma Cannon/Laser Trip Bombs	812A5AC20101

EXTREME-G

All Tracks and Bonus Cars

For all tracks and bonus cars, enter the password 81GGD5.

Boulder Dash

Start a new Contest and press R Shift at the Bike Selection screen. When the name prompt appears, press R Shift again and enter your name as roller.

Extreme Speed

Enter your name as xtreme.

Transparent Track

Enter your name as ghostly.

Fisheye Lens

Enter your name as fisheye.

Magnify Mode

Enter your name as magnify.

Race as the Extreme Team

Enter your name as XGTEAM. Go back and change the name to the first name of one of the game's programmers.

Race Upside Down

Enter your name as antigrav.

Random Weapons

Enter your name as arsenal.

Shoot Fergus

Enter your name as FERGUS, then enter the Shoot 'em Up Mode.

Slippery Track

Enter your name as banana.

Stealth Mode

Enter your name as stealth.

Ugly Mode

Enter your name as uglymode.

Unlimited Turbo Boosts

Enter your name as nitroid.

Win by Quitting

Enter your name as RA50. Quit at any time during the race and you will still be credited with the win.

Wireframe Mode

Enter your name as wired.

GameShark Codes

EFFECT	CODE
100 Points	80167C370063
Anti-Grav and Fish Eye Lens	80095F6F000A
Anti-Gravity Mode	80095F6F0008
Boulder Mode	80095F6F0001
Boulder Mode and Fish Eye Lens	80095F6F0003
Boulder Mode and Wireframe Mode	80095F6F0011
Extreme Mode	80095F6E0002
Fish Eye Lens	80095F6F0002
Ghost Mode	80095F6F0040
Infinite Turbos	801635CB0003
Infinite Turbos	801635CF0003
Magnify Mode	80095F6F0004
Stealth Mode	80095F6F0020
Ugly Mode	80095F6F0080
Wireframe Mode	80095F6F0010

FIFA: ROAD TO THE WORLD CUP '98

At the Player Edit screen, select the following Team and enter the corresponding Player's Name.

Effect	Team	Player's Name
Australia Mode (Upside Down)	OFC/Australia	NWODEDISPU

Effect	Team	Player's Name
Feedback Preview	AFC/Japan	NORIE
(*At the Round Select screen (RTWC), press Z + C-Left + C-Up)		
Hot Potato Mode	UEFA/Rep. Of Ireland	SPUD
Invisible Walls	UEFA/Wales	WARREN
Unlimited Player Points	USA/Vancouver	DAVE
Road to the World Cup Round 2	AFC/Japan	YUJI
Upside Down Mode	USA/Vancouver	TED
Ghost Players	UEFA/Slovakia	LASKO
Invisible Players	England/SheffieldW	WAYNE
Pencil and Paper Mode	CONCACAF/Canada	MARC

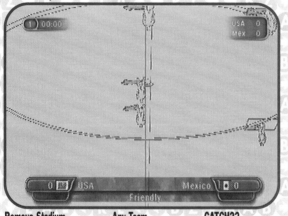

Remove Stadium	Any Team	CATCH22
Tiny Players	USA/Vancouver	KERRY

GameShark Codes

EFFECT	CODE
Away Team Scores 0	801190430000
Away Team Scores 9	801190430009
Home Team Scores 0	801190470000
Home Team Scores 9	801190470009

FIGHTER'S DESTINY

Play as Robert the Robot

Go into the Fastest Mode and beat all the fighters in less than one minute (combined time). This will enable you to play as Robert.

NOTE: You may have to use a character with a star to get this trick to work. You can earn a star by defeating the game.

Play as Ushi the Cow

Enter the Rodeo Mode and stay alive for one minute (or more). Doing so enables you to select the Cow as a playable character. There are even two colors from which to choose: brown and "classic" cow.

NOTE: You may have to use a character with a star to get this trick to work. You can earn a star by defeating the game.

Play as the Joker

To play as the Joker, defeat all 100 characters in the Survival Mode.

NOTE: You may have to use a character with a star to get this trick to work. You can earn a star by defeating the game.

Play as the Master

Enter the Master Challenge using any character and defeat everyone. This enables you to select the Master as a playable character.

9th Skill

After getting all of the eight skills from Master Mode, select a 2-player battle. Choose Win or Lose and pick the player for which you have the eight skills. Defeat your opponent and they will lose a skill, enabling you to gain a 9th skill.

Character	9th Skill	Movement
Ryuji	Rock Crasher	Forward, Down/Forward, Down, B
Abdul	Poison Hand	Up, B, Forward, B
Pierre	Quick Middle	Back, B
Leon	Back Knuckle Melt	Down/Back, B, B, A
Tomahawk	Throw Reserve	Forward, Forward, B + A
Meiling	Butterfly Clean	Forward, B, A
Valerie	Elbow Twist Thrust	B
Bob	Elbow Twist Right	Back, Forward, B, B, B
Ninja	True Hidden Feet	A, B, Forward + B
Boro	Plain Step Low	Forward, A, B, A

GameShark Codes

EFFECT	CODE
Player 1 Always Has 0 Stars	802097570000
Player 1 Start w/ Extra Stars	D02097570000
Player 1 Start w/ Extra Stars	80209757000F
Player 2 Always Has 0 Stars	8020B61F0000
Player 2 Start w/ Extra Stars	D020B61F0000
Player 2 Start w/ Extra Stars	8020B61F000F

FORSAKEN

Gore Mode

At the Press Start screen, press Z, Down, C-Up, C-Left, C-Left, C-Left, C-Left, C-Down.

Psychedelic Mode

At the Press Start screen, press A, R Shift, Left, Right, Down, C-Up, C-Left, C-Down.

Turbo Crazy Mode

At the Press Start screen, press B, B, Right Shift, Up, Left, Down, C-Up, C-left. This will give you unlimited nitro boosts.

Wire-Frame Mode

At the Press Start screen, press L Shift, L Shift, R Shift, Z, Left, Right, C-Up, C-Right.

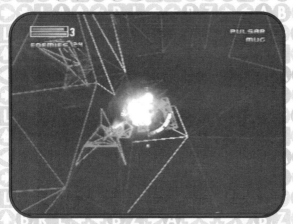

GOLDENEYE 007

Every Multiplayer Character

At the Multiplayer Character Select screen, do the following:

1. Hold L Shift + R Shift and press C-Left.
2. Hold L Shift and press C-Up.
3. Hold L Shift + R Shift and press Left on the D-Pad. (This should select another character.)
4. Hold L Shift and press Right on the D-Pad.
5. Hold R Shift and press Down on the D-Pad.
6. Hold L Shift + R Shift and press C-Left.
7. Hold L Shift and press C-Up.
8. Hold L Shift + R Shift and press Right on the D-Pad.
9. Hold L Shift + R Shift and press C-Down.
10. Hold L Shift and press Down on the D-Pad.

You should now be able to select from 66 characters instead of the usual 33. This code will not be saved, so you will need to reenter this code every time you reset.

GameShark Codes

Cheat Options

To access these GameShark cheats, you must already have obtained the Cheat Options menu. The easiest level to do this on is the Runway level.

EFFECT	CODE
All Guns	800696530001
Invisible Bond	8006965A0001
DK Mode	8006965C0001
Enemy Rockets	8006966C0001
Fast Animation	8006966A0001
Infinite Ammo	8006965B0001
Invincible	800696520001
Line Mode	800696570001
No Radar (Multi)	800696670001
Paint Ball Mode	8006965F0001
Slow Animation	8006966B0001
Tiny Bond	8006965E0001
Turbo Mode	800696680001

Multiplayer Codes

You can only use one of the following codes at a time.

EFFECT	CODE
More Characters	8002B1970040
Play Egyptian Level w/4 Players	8002B537000B
Play Caverns Level w/4 Players	8002B537000A
Play Archives Level w/4 Players	8002B5370009
Play Bunker Level w/4 Players	8002B5370008

Level Codes

To access the following codes, you must first turn off all other codes.

EFFECT	CODE
Extra Ammo	80030B280042
Bulletproof Bond	8002CE440030
	80030B200030
Enemy Cannot Aim	8002CE400030
	80030B1C0030
Weak Enemies	8002CE480048

HEXEN

Cheat Menu

Pause the game and press C-Up, C-Down, C-Left, C-Right. The word "Cheat" will appear at the bottom of the menu when entered correctly. Now you can enter the following:

EFFECT	CODE
God Mode	C-Left, C-Right, C-Down
Walk through walls	C-Up (x20), C-Down
Level Select	C-Left, C-Left, C-Right, C-Right, C-Down, C-Up
Kill all enemies on-screen	C-Down, C-Up, C-Left, C-Left
Full Health	C-Left, C-Up, C-Down, C-Down

The following appear under the Collect option:

EFFECT	CODE
All Keys	C-Down, C-Up, C-Left, C-Right
All Artifacts	C-Up, C-Right, C-Down, C-Up
All Weapons	C-Right, C-Up, C-Down, C-Down
Puzzle Items	C-Up, C-Left (x3), C-Right, C-Down (x2)

GameShark Codes

EFFECT	CODE
Infinite Blue Mana	8013DB7D00CF
Infinite Green Mana	8013DB7F00CF
Invincibility	8113DB4CFFFF

IN THE ZONE '98
GameShark Codes

EFFECT	CODE
Away Team Scores 0 points	8013C2B30000
Away Team Scores 150 points	8013C2B30096
Home Team Scores 0 points	8013C2B10000
Home Team Scores 150 points	8013C2B10096

KILLER INSTINCT GOLD
GameShark Codes

EFFECT	CODE
Player 1 Fast Jump/Walk	801D347C0001
Player 1 Slow Jump/Walk	801D347D0050
Player 1 Unlimited Energy	801D34840069
Player 1 Untouchable	801D34D4000A
Player 1 Fast Punch Kick	801D347E0010

KOBE BRYANT IN NBA COURTSIDE

Hidden Teams

To access the hidden teams, hold L Shift while selecting Pre-Season. This unveils the following new teams: Nintendo Gamers, Nintendo Plumbers, and Left Field Lefties.

Hang on Rim

After a 2-handed jam, you can press and hold B to hang on the rim longer. Hang too long, though, and you'll get called for a technical foul.

Disco Floor Code

During gameplay, pause the game and press A, C-Up, Down, Up, C-Down, R Shift, R Shift, B, C-Right, C-Right, Z.

MACE: THE DARK AGE

Play As War Mech & Ichiro

At the legal screen, press Down, Right, Up, Left. You will hear a "swoosh" sound when the code is entered correctly. War Mech and Ichiro will appear in the Character Select screen until you reset the game.

Play As Ned

At the Character Select screen, highlight Koyasha and press Start, highlight the Executioner and press Start, then highlight Lord Deimos and press Start. Then go to Xiao Long and press A or B to select Ned.

A
B
C
D
E
F
G
H
I
J
K
L
M
N
O
P
Q
R
S
T
U
V
W
X
Y
Z

Play As Grendal

To play as Grendal, you must win four times in a 1-player match or three times in a 2-player match. Then at the Character Select screen, press and hold Start while on the Executioner. While still holding Start, press A or B to select Grendal.

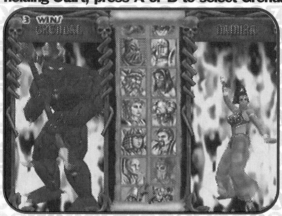

Fight at Mini Golf Course

At the Character Select screen, highlight Koyasha and press Start, highlight Mordos Kull and press Start, and then highlight Takeshi and press Start.

Play As Pojo

Perform Taria's Fatality during a match. Then at the Character Select screen, press and hold Start on Taria. Then, while still holding Start, press A or B to select Pojo.

A
B
C
D
E
F
G
H
I
J
K
L
M
N
O
P
Q
R
S
T
U
V
W
X
Y
Z

Fight at Machu Pichu

At the Character Select screen, highlight Namira and press Start, highlight Koyasha and press Start, and then highlight Taria and press Start.

Bunny Slippers

At the Character Select screen, highlight Ragnar and press Start, highlight Dregan and press Start, and then Highlight Koyasha and press Start.

Change Heads

At the Character Select screen, highlight Al-Rashid and press Start, highlight Takeshi and press Start, highlight Mordos Kull and press Start, highlight Xiao Long and press Start, and then highlight Namira and press Start.

Big Heads

At the Character Select screen, highlight Ragnar and press Start, highlight Al-Rashid and press Start, and then highlight Takeshi and press Start.

Little Fighters

At the Character Select screen, highlight Takeshi and press Start, highlight Al-Rashid and press Start, highlight Ragnar and press Start, and then highlight Xiao Long and press Start.

Random AI

At the Character Select screen, highlight Hell Knight and press Start, highlight Xiao Long and press Start, highlight Dregan and press Start, and then highlight Namira and press Start.

Different Color Palettes

To change the color palettes of the characters, press C-Up, C-Down, C-Right, or C-Left.

Level Select

To play on a particular level, highlight a character whose board you want to fight on and press Start four times, then select your character.

GameShark Codes

EFFECT	CODE
Infinite Health Player 1	8008B1E70064
Infinite Health Player 2	8008AE5F0064
No Health Player 1	8008B1E70000
No Health Player 2	8008AE5F0000
Extra Characters	8007F9F80001
R Button Health	D007CD2B0010
Restore Player 1	8008B1E70064
Z Trigger	D007CD2A0020
Deathblow Player 1	8008AE5F0000

MADDEN FOOTBALL 64

Tiburon Team

At the Create Player screen, enter the name TIBURON. Select Continue and Save, then press B twice to return to the Main menu. Select Exhibition Mode and you should see the Tiburon Team now available.

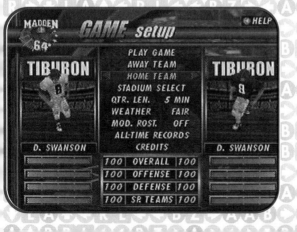

EA Team

At the Create Player screen, enter the name **ELEC ARTS**. Select Continue and Save, and then press B twice to return to the Main menu. Select Exhibition Mode and you should see the EA team now available.

Stats Leaders Team

At the Create Player screen, enter the name **STATS MEN**. Select Continue and Save, and then press B twice to return to the Main menu. Select Exhibition Mode and you should see the Stats Leaders team now available.

1960 Conference B Team

At the Create Player screen, enter the name **SIXTIES**. Select Continue and Save, and then press B twice to return to the Main menu. Select Exhibition Mode and you should see the 1960 Conference B team now available.

All 70s Team

At the Create Player screen, enter the name SEVENTIES. Select Continue and Save, and then press B twice to return to the Main menu. Select Exhibition Mode and you should see the All 70s team now available.

All 80s Team

At the Create Player screen, enter the name EIGHTIES. Select Continue and Save, and then press B twice to return to the Main menu. Select Exhibition Mode and you should see the All 80s team now available.

1997 Conference A Team

At the Create Player screen, enter the name HOWLIE. Select Continue and Save, and then press B twice to return to the Main menu. Select Exhibition Mode and you should see the 97 Conference A team now available.

1997 Conference B Team

At the Create Player screen, enter the name LEI. Select Continue and Save, and then press B twice to return to the Main menu. Select Exhibition Mode and you should see the 97 Conference B team now available.

A
B
C
D
E
F
G
H
I
J
K
L
M
N
O
P
Q
R
S
T
U
V
W
X
Y
Z

Tiburon Stadium

At the Create Player screen, enter the name MAITLAND. Select Continue and Save, and then press B twice to return to the Main menu. The Tiburon Stadium should now be available.

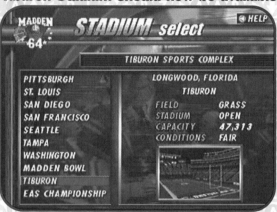

EA Sports Stadium

At the Create Player screen, enter the name SAN MATEO. Select Continue and Save, and then press B twice to return to the Main menu. The EA Sports Stadium should now be available.

View Ending Sequences

Turn on the N64 system and hold L Shift, R Shift, and the Z trigger when the EA logo appears.

High-Steppin'

When a player is in the clear and nearing the endzone for a touchdown, press and hold C-Left. Now sit back and watch as your player struts his stuff down the sidelines. Prime Time, baby!

GameShark Codes

EFFECT	CODES
Infinite Time-outs Home Team	80082D970003
Infinite Time-outs Away Team	80084EE30003

MAJOR LEAGUE BASEBALL FEATURING KEN GRIFFEY JR.

Secret Teams

Highlight Exhibition at the first menu. Continuously press all four C buttons until you hear a beep. You should find two new teams, Nintendo and Angel Studios, on the same screens where the All-Star teams are located.

Spin Baseball on Title Screen

At the Title screen, hold the Z trigger to stop the baseball. While holding Z, you can move the joystick to make the baseball rotate in different directions.

Shoot Fireworks

When selecting your stadium, press Z to view the stadium. Then press Z + R Shift to shoot fireworks from home plate.

View Ending

Choose an Exhibition game and select your team. At the Stadium Select screen, press all four C-buttons until you hear a beep. Press Z to view the stadium and you will see the ending.

MARIO KART 64

GameShark Codes

EFFECT	CODE
No Laps to Race	811643900000
No Laps to Race	811643920002

MORTAL KOMBAT 4

Cheat Menu

At the Options screen, highlight Continues, then hold Block and Run for 10 seconds.

Play as Noob Saibot

At the Character Select screen, choose the Hidden option, then go up two and over one to Reiko. Then press Run and Block.

Play As Goro

At the Character Select screen, choose the Hidden option, then go up three and over one to Shinnok. Then press Run and Block.

Hidden Uniforms

To access each character's hidden uniforms and weapons, perform the following: At the Character Select screen, press and hold the Start button. While still holding the Start button, press either the Punch or Kick buttons. Each time you press one of the buttons, your character's picture will spin. Each spin gives you access to one of the new uniform/new weapon combinations. Refer to the following chart to determine which uniform or weapon you will get. Note that some characters DO NOT have new uniforms; in place of the uniforms are different weapons.

Scorpion

Spin (X1)	Spin (X2)	Spin (X3)
Original Arcade	Smoke Uniform & Mace Club	Curved Blade & Alternate Uniform

Rayden

Spin (X1)	Spin (X2)	Spin (X3)
Original Arcade	MKII Uniform & Blade Wheel	Alternate Uniform & Kali Dagger

Kai

Spin (X1)	Spin (X2)	Spin (X3)
Original Arcade	Rayden Staff	Biker Gear & Spiked Club

Reptile

Spin (X1)	Spin (X2)	Spin (X3)
Original Arcade	MKII Uniform	Spiked Club

Johnny Cage

Spin (X1)	Spin (X2)	Spin (X3)
Original Arcade	Kali Dagger	Tux & Gun

Tanya

Spin (X1)	Spin (X2)	Spin (X3)
Original Arcade	Ice Wand	Black Dress & Hammer

Reiko

Spin (X1)	Spin (X2)	Spin (X3)
Original Arcade	Dragon Sword	Alternate Uniform & Crossbow

A
B
C
D
E
F
G
H
I
J
K
L
M
N
O
P
Q
R
S
T
U
V
W
X
Y
Z

Jax

Spin (X1)	Spin (X2)	Spin (X3)
Original Arcade	White Uniform & Spear	Kali Dagger

Jarek

Spin (X1)	Spin (X2)	Spin (X3)
Original Arcade	Wood Hammer	Wood Hammer

Quan Chi

Spin (X1)	Spin (X2)	Spin (X3)
Original Arcade	Wide Blade	Alternate Uniform & Crossbow

Fujin

Spin (X1)	Spin (X2)	Spin (X3)
Original Arcade	Spiked Club	Spear & Alternate Uniform

Sub-Zero

Spin (X1)	Spin (X2)	Spin (X3)
Original Arcade	Frozen Uniform & Ax	Dragon Sword & Alternate Uniform

Shinnok

Spin (X1)	Spin (X2)	Spin (X3)
Original Arcade	Broad Sword	Alternate Uniform & Boomerang

Lui Kang

Spin (X1)	Spin (X2)	Spin (X3)
Original Arcade	Karate Uniform	Alternate Uniform

Sonya Blade

Spin (X1)	Spin (X2)	Spin (X3)
Original Arcade	Kali Dagger	Purple Uniform & Mace Club

VS Kodes

In a 2-player match, you can enter codes that will alter the gameplay in some way. To enter the codes, you must mix and match a set of six icons. Each player controls three of the six icons. Player 1 controls the first three, while Player 2 controls the last three. You can change the icons by pressing Low Punch for the first icon, Block for the second icon, and Low Kick for the third icon. You can also hold up on the joystick while entering these codes—this toggles the icons backwards.

In the table below, the *Player 1* and *Player 2* columns indicate the number of times the player must press each of the three buttons which correspond to the three icons he or she controls. For example, to enter the *Randper Kombat* code, the table indicates *3,3,3* for both Player 1 and Player 2. This means that both players must tap all three of their buttons (LP, BL, and LK) three times.

Lastly, the final column lists the effect, name, or stage for each code.

Player 1	Player 2	EFFECT
123	123	1-hit Win
012	012	Noob Saibot Mode
020	020	Red Rain (perform on the Rain stage)
050	050	Explosive Kombat
002	002	Weapon drawn but can't be knocked out of character's hands
100	100	Disable throws
010	010	Disable Max Damage
110	110	No Throw/Disable Max Damage
111	111	Free weapon (Random weapon falls)

Player 1	Player 2	EFFECT
222	222	Start with random weapon
333	333	Randper Kombat
444	444	Start with weapons drawn
555	555	Many weapons
666	666	Silent Kombat
321	321	Big Head Mode
011	011	Goro Lair (Spike Pit)
022	022	The Well (Scorpion's Stage)
033	033	Elder Gods (Blue Face)
044	044	The Tomb Stage
055	055	The Rain Stage
066	066	Snake Stage

A B C D E F G H I J K L M N O P Q R S T U V W X Y Z

Player 1	Player 2	EFFECT
101	101	Shaolin Temple
202	202	Living Forest
303	303	Prison (Fan Stage)
313	313	Ice Pit Level

Play as Meat

In a 2-player game, go to Group mode and then win with all the characters on the Select screen. This will enable you to have Meat at your control. His moves mirror those of the character you've highlighted with the red box on the Character Select screen.

MORTAL KOMBAT MYTHOLOGIES: SUB-ZERO

Passwords

Level	Password
Wind	THWMSB
Earth	CNSZDG
Water	ZVRKDM
Fire	JYPPHD
Prison	RGTKCS
Bridge	QFTLWN
Fortress	XJKNZT

Enter the following codes at the Password screen.

Credits
CRVDTS

Urn of Vitalities
NXCVSZ

Fortress w/20K
ZCHRRY

If Sub-Zero dies once before reaching any of the checkpoints, hold A as he dies and you'll go directly to the Quan Chi fight. Hold B and you'll go directly to Shinnok's stage.

1,000 Lives
GTTBHR

GameShark Code

EFFECT	CODE
Infinite Lives	8010BCFF0005

MORTAL KOMBAT TRILOGY

GameShark Code

EFFECT	CODE
Player 1 Unlimited Energy	8016984D00A6
Player 1 No Energy	8016984D0000
Player 2 No Energy	80169B210000
Player 2 Unlimited Energy	80169B2100A6

MULTI RACING CHAMPIONSHIP

Match Race Mode

Place first in all of the difficulty levels in Championship Mode to open up Match Race Mode.

Bonus Cars

After defeating every course in Match Race, you will face your first opponent. Defeat this racer and you can race in that car against the second challenger. Defeat this racer to use this car and win the Match Race Mode.

GameShark Code

EFFECT	CODE
Always Place 1st	800A960F0000
Infinite Time	80094E970064
	D0094E97000A
Low Course Time	8009483B0000

MYSTICAL NINJA STARRING GOEMON

Consecutive Fighting Large Boss Mode

Find all of the cats in the game and a new option will appear in the options menu called Consecutive Fighting Large Boss Mode. Enter this mode to play the four Impact scenarios against the Bosses.

NAGANO WINTER OLYMPICS '98

Ski on Your Head

Select Olympic Mode and then Freestyle Aerials. Don't press any button until you leave the ramp, then rapidly press the B button. When done correctly, the skier will flip on his head and ski down the rest of the slope.

GameShark Codes

EFFECT	CODE
Infinite Stamina	81138400447A
	81138404447A
Start Resets Timer	811378860000

NFL QUARTERBACK CLUB '98

Enter the following at the Enter Cheat screen:

Effect	Code
Huge players	GLYTHMD

Tiny players   **SMLMDGT**

Tall and skinny   **BBMNTBL**

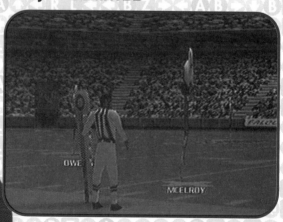

Short, wide, and flattened JPNSMWR

Better Quarterbacks   BRDWYNMTH
Better Running Backs   WLTRPYTN
8 Downs   DWNDRV

Faster players   MCHLJNSN
Super jumps   CRLLWYS

Stronger and Faster	**BGBFYFF**
Better defense	**BGBFYDF**
Slower but very difficult to bring down	**RNLDSWZNGR**
Fumble	**GTNHNDS**

STATS—OVERALL		
△0	SAFETIES FOR	0
17	TAKEAWAYS	28
28	GIVEAWAYS	17
1/0	OFFENSE PENALTIES	0/0
8/100	DEFENSE PENALTIES	5/65
52	FUMBLES	36
37	FUMBLES RECOVERED	47
10:48	TIME OF POSS.	09:12

Slippery Play	**SPRSLYD**

Improved Catching **STYCKYHNDS**

Maxed out abilities for all teams **SPRTMMD**

Players slide around in sitting position **SNWSLDS**

No turnovers **TGHTGRP**

Gameplay in extreme slow motion **FRMBYFRM**

Player with ball continuously spins **BGTWSTRS**

Players have maxed out arm strength **SPRBGRMS**

A
B
C
D
E
F
G
H
I
J
K
L
M
N
O
P
Q
R
S
T
U
V
W
X
Y
Z

Easier tackling	**SPRDPRTCKL**
Field mines make movement difficult	**MNFLDMD**
Players awareness and discipline maxed out	**YNSTYNS**
Players dive further	**BGSPRDV**
Players slide on one foot	**YLCTRCFB**
Poor offensive play	**LLFFSCK**
Poor defensive play	**LLDFSCK**
Players crawl like babies	**PBYBYMD**

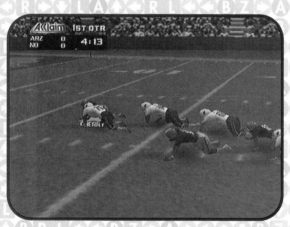

Computer won't tackle ball carrier	**NBCTCKLS**
Turns off cheats	**LLCHTSFF**
Ball appears in player's hands the instant it's thrown	**LDSTRTRK**
Opponent always tips ball on passing plays	**LWYSTPSS**

NHL BREAKAWAY '98

New Teams

Press C-Up, Left, and C-Left as you select your team. You will hear the sound of the puck hitting the stick when entered correctly.

Cheat Menu

At the Main menu press C-Left, C-Right, C-Left, C-Right, R Shift, R Shift. A Cheat Menu should now be selectable.

Perfect Player

Enter the name Jim Jung at the Create A Player screen for a perfect player.

100 Bonus Points in Season Mode

At the Main Season menu, press C-Left, C-Left, C-Right, C-Right, C-Left, C-Left, C-Right, C-Right, R Shift. You can repeat this code multiple times.

OLYMPIC HOCKEY NAGANO '98

Debug Mode

At the Options screen, press C-Down + R Shift, C-Left + R Shift or C-Up + R Shift. When done correctly, a window appears at the bottom of the screen that enables you to modify a 16-bit register.

You can only change the first 6 bits. To alter the bits, use the following controls:

C-Down + R Shift:	Changes the first two bits
C-Left + R Shift:	Changes the third and fourth bits
C-Up + R Shift:	Changes the fifth and sixth bits

The following are a few combinations:

100000:	Stocky Players
010000:	Stocky Players, Big Heads
110000:	Stocky Players, Small Heads
001000:	Small Players, Small Announcer
000100:	Large Players, Large Announcer

000010:	Crunched Players, Small Announcer
000001:	Elongated Players, Large Announcer
110110:	Large Players, Small Heads, Large Announcer
010010:	Crunched Players, Large Heads, Small Announcer
010101:	Large Players, Large Heads, Large Announcer
010001:	Elongated Players, Large Heads, Large Announcer

More Fighting

At the Options screen, highlight Fighting and hold L Shift and press C-Right, C-Left, C-Left, C-Right, C-Down, C-Up, C-Up, C-Down, C-Left, C-Right, C-Right, C-Left, C-Right, C-Left.

NBA HANGTIME

GameShark Codes

EFFECT	CODE
Press GS Button for 99 Points (Player 1)	890a66890063 890a668b0063

PILOT WINGS

GameShark Codes

EFFECT	CODE
Infinite fuel for Gyrocopter	803628210081
Low Timer	803627500001

QUAKE 64

Debug Mode

Enter all Q's as the password. This will give you a level select, God Mode, Weapons, and a Target toggle.

Walk Through Walls

Enter NOCLIP at the password screen.

Passwords

Level	Password
Level 2: Castle of the Damned	H40X ZVVB HLBD 74DJ
Level 3: The Necropolis	HOP3 2XBN WQ2B NZVK
Level 4: Gloom Keep	CWHX CH3B GDB3 14JY
Level 5: The Door to Chthon	PQW4 9QVD Y8VY X21M
Level 6: The House of Chthon	PL24 XBBT YJLQ 32?6
Level 7: Ziggurat Vertigo (Secret Level)	6JR3 KDDV 3SLG 9RFT
Level 8: The Ogre Citadel	GWY6 7BBB 23BD L4HK
Level 9: The Crypt of Decay	B8YN BBBB ZBBB SXR4
Level 10: The Wizard's Manse	55R6 0XCJ 2LBR QVV1
Level 11: The Dismal Oubliette	51RZ ?6xQ RGBR NNJH
Level 12: Underearth (Secret Level)	5XRV SMXP B7BR LP5H
Level 13: Termination Central	5SR9 TPFG VQBR JBCT
Level 14: Vaults of Zin	5NRV JF6G CVBR GBFL
Level 15: The Tomb of Terror	5JR6 HDXM 2ZBR DPN5
Level 16: Satan's Dark Delight	5DRO HW4N PZ?S 5Y2W
Level 17: Chambers of Torment	49R6 XBBJ 2GBQ 932T

Level 18: The Haunted Halls (Secret Level)	45RZ ZF32 LZBQ 773R
Level 19: The Tower of Despair	41R0 6PFG WGBQ 5BCH
Level 20: The Elder God Shrine	4XRV QBFG B3BQ 3BD3
Level 21: The Palace of Hate	4SR5 DBBN ZGBQ 1628
Level 22: The Pain Maze	4NRV JBBF BRY5 744W
Level 23: Azure Agony	4JR5 1BBB 0QBQ X4HX
Level 24: Shub-Niggurath's Pit	39R9 2PFG W7BQ SBCF
Level 25: The Nameless City (Secret Level)	4DR1 4XDD RVBQ VM1B

GameShark Codes

EFFECT	CODE
Infinite Ammo	80163A2D0064
	80163A2F0064
	80163A310064
	80163A330064
All Weapons	801639EB007F
Debug Mode	8006C4C20001

RAMPAGE: WORLD TOUR

Level Select

At the Character Select screen, hold L Shift + R Shift + Z and all the C buttons, and then start a new game. When the screen says "Peoria Day 1," press Up or Down to choose your country and Left or Right to choose your city.

Hidden Cities

To access the hidden cities, rapidly punch one of the buttons on-screen that appears below your next city.

Character	Button
George	Jump
Lizzie	Punch
Ralph	Kick

City	Destination
San Diego	Caleb's City
Fairbanks	Underworld
Atlanta	Suburbia
Louisville	Warehouse
Phoenix	Area 69

Game Shark Codes

EFFECT	CODE
Infinite Health Player 1	800BF86C0064
Infinite Health Player 2	800BFA380064
Infinite Health Player 3	800BFC040064

ROBOTRON 64

50 Extra Lives

At the Setup menu press Up, Up, Down, Down, Left, Right, Left, Right, C-Left, C-Right, C-Left, C-Right.

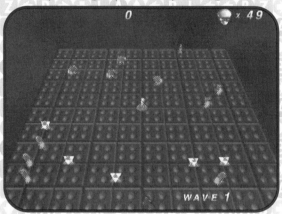

2-Color Mode

At the Setup menu press Up, Down, Right, C-Left, Down, Up, Left, C-Right, Up, Down.

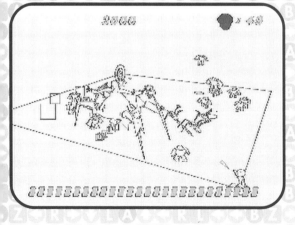

Level Select

At the Setup menu press Down, Up, C-Left, Down, C-Left, C-Right, Down, C-Right.

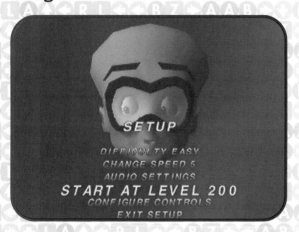

Shield

During gameplay, press Down, Left, C-Left, C-Right.

Speed Up

During gameplay, press Left, Left, Right, Right, C-Up.

Two-Way Fire

During gameplay, press Up, C-Up, Up, C-Up.

Three-Way Fire

During gameplay, press Right, Right, C-Left, C-Down.

Four-Way Fire
During gameplay, press Down, Down, Up, C-Right.

Gas Gun
During gameplay, press Up, Down, C-Right, C-Left.

Flame Thrower
During gameplay, press Down, Right, Down, Right, C-Right.

GameShark Codes

EFFECT	CODE
Infinite Lives Player 1	8009S0009

SAN FRANCISCO RUSH

Turn Cones into Mines
At the Setup screen, press L Shift, R Shift, L Shift, R Shift, L Shift, R Shift.

Upside Down Tracks

At the Setup screen, press Up, Right, Down, Left, Down, Right, Up, Left.

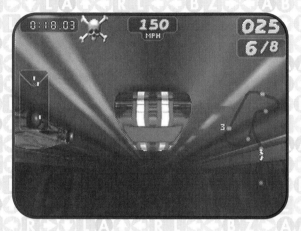

Foggy Night

At the Options screen, change "Fog" to the "Heavy" setting. Then hold all four C buttons and press Right on the D-pad.

Auto Abort Disable
At the Setup screen, press C-Up, C-Up, C-Up, C-Up.

Change Car Size
At the Car Select screen, press and hold C-Down and then C-Up and release both buttons. Then press and hold C-Up then C-Down and release both buttons to activate the code. Repeat the code to get a new size.

Change Fog Color
At the Car Select screen, press and hold the Z trigger and press C-Down, C-Down, C-Down.

Change Front Tire Size
At the Car Select screen, press and hold C-Left, then C-Right. Release both buttons. Press and hold C-Right, then C-Left, then release both buttons to activate the code.

Change Rear Tire Size
At the Car Select screen, press and hold C-Right, then C-Left and release both buttons. Press and hold C-Left, then C-Right to activate the code.

A B C D E F G H I J K L M N O P Q R S T U V W X Y Z

Change Gravity

At the Setup screen, hold the Z trigger and press Up, Down. Release the Z trigger and press Up, Down, Up, Down.

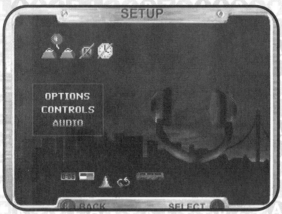

Change Track Textures

At the Setup screen, press and hold C-Right, then press L Shift. Release both buttons, then press the Z trigger. Press and hold C-Right, then press L Shift and release both buttons. Press the Z trigger again to activate the code.

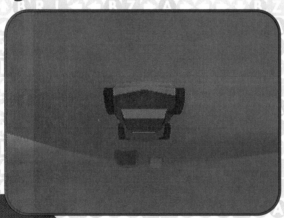

Disable Vehicle Collisions

At the Setup screen, press Left, then hold Right, and then press C-Right and release both buttons. Press C-Up, C-Left, C-Down, Z.

Drive an Exploding Hulk

At the Car Select screen, hold C-Up and press Z (x4).

Infinite Time

At the Setup screen, hold Z, then press and hold C-Down, then C-Up. Continue to hold the Z trigger, and release the C buttons. Press and hold C-Up, then C-Down to activate the code.

Resurrect in Place

At the Setup screen, hold the Z trigger, then hold C-Left and then C-Right. Continue to hold the Z trigger, and release the C buttons. Press and hold C-Right, then C-Left to activate the code.

Reverse Controls

At the Options screen, highlight Mirror and hold all four C buttons. Press Left or Right to view an extra option called Extreme.

Tag Mode

To access Tag Mode, hit the Abort button during the countdown sequence at the start of a 2-player practice game.

Turn Car into Mine

At the Car Select screen, press C-Right, C-Right, Z, C-Down, C-Up, Z, C-Left, C-Left.

Alcatraz

Note: If you've already completed a circuit and have it saved to a Controller Pak, you can bypass the codes below and skip straight to the four steps to obtain the track.

First, you'll need to finish a circuit. To save you the time of doing that, Atari has included the circuit winning code as follows:

8DP5KG5L4G59P

G92WVCQY0DRDQ

NOTE: Japanese (in addition to a rare few US and European) carts may require this alternative code to work:

9DQ6LH6M5H6$Q

H$3XWCR01DTDR

Once you've done that, choose the option to continue circuit and then let the time run out while racing. After a quick congratulation screen (and the reward code for the Formula 1 car) you can get started.

Alcatraz—Track 7 (only allowed if you've finished a circuit)

1.   **On car select screen: Hold C-Left, press Z, release both, press Left**

2.   **On setup screen: Hold C-Up, press Z, release both, press Up**

3.   **On track select screen: Hold C-Right, press Z, release both, press Right**

4.   **On car select screen: Hold C-Down, press Z, release both, press Down, L, R**

If you have a memory pak you can save Alcatraz (track 7) as follows:

1.   **Enter circuit code (above) to continue a circuit.**

2.   **Finish race/die/let time run out.**

3.   **Start a new game (without using a player, to tell system you've completed a circuit).**

4.   **Go to the car select screen and enter first part of code.**

5.   **Back up to the setup screen and enter second part of code.**

6.   **Start a new game, this time selecting a Pak player.**

7. Go to car select screen and enter final part of code.

8. Start game and track 7 is saved/enabled under current player.

GameShark Codes

EFFECT	CODE
Change Textures	800F3DA00001
Cones to Mines	800F3F880001
Upside-down Mode	800F40610001
Resurrect In Place	800F40800001
Auto Abort Disable	800F40780001
Fat Cars	800F40B10002
Flat Cars	800F40B10001
Giant Cars	800F40B10003
No Collisions	800F40500001
Stop Timer	800F40900001

SNOWBOARD KIDS

All Tracks and Hidden Character Sinobin

At the Title screen, press Down, Up, Down, Up, C-Down, C-Up, L Shift, R Shift, Z, Left, C-Right, Up, B, Right, C-Left, Start. You should hear Nancy say "Yeah."

- ROOKIE MT.
- BIG SNOWMAN
- SUNSET ROCK
- NIGHT HIGHWAY
- GRASS VALLEY
- DIZZY-LAND
- QUICKSAND VALLEY
- SILVER MT.
- NINJA LAND
- RETURN TO MENU

COURSE

LENGTH
382 m
DIFFICULTY
★ ★

LAP 1 / 9

4

A
B
C
D
E
F
G
H
I
J
K
L
M
N
O
P
Q
R
S
T
U
V
W
X
Y
Z

Quicksand Valley
(7th Course)

Finish in first place on the first 6 courses.

Silver Mountain
(8th Course)

Finish in first place on Quicksand Valley.

Ninja Mountain
(9th Course)

Finish in first place on Silver Mountain.

Ninja Character Sinobin

Finish in first place on Ninja Mountain.

GameShark Codes

EFFECT	CODE
Infinite cash	801222EAc350
1 lap race	D01222880000
	801222880009

STAR FOX 64

Game Shark Codes

EFFECT	CODE
Hyper Laser	8015791b0002
Infinite armor	8013ab2700ff
Infinite armor	80137c4700ff
Lots of hits	8015790b00ff

Unlimited Lives (Player 1)	801579110040
Unlimited Smart Bombs (Player 1)	8016dc130004
Infinite armor (Peppy)	8016d72f00ff
Infinite armor (Slippy)	8016d72b00ff
Infinite armor (Falco)	8016d72700ff

STAR WARS: SHADOWS OF THE EMPIRE

Play as a Wampa, Stormtrooper, or AT-ST

Start a new game and enter your name as _Wampa__Stompa (note that there is one space before Wampa and two spaces between Wampa and Stompa). This is also case-sensitive—you must capitalize the "W" and "S." Make sure your controller is set to traditional setting and start a game. You can now do the following:

Play through the Battle of Hoth until the AT-STs appear. At the same time, press Left on the D-Pad and C-Right and then press Up on the D-pad. Use C-Right to scroll through the camera views. The "behind-the-ship-view" is replaced with a view behind an AT-ST. Use the D-Pad to move the AT-ST and press Up to fire.

In Escape from Echo Base, press Left and C-Right at the same time and then press Up. Use C-Right to switch between Dash and the Wampa; use the D-pad to move; press Down to swipe.

At the beginning of Space Freighter, press Left and C-Right at the same time and then press Up. Use C-Right to switch between Dash and the Stormtrooper; use the D-pad to move; press Down to fire your blaster.

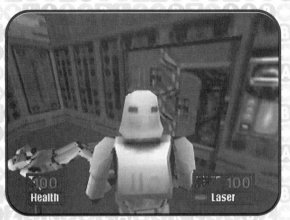

Fly the X-Wing or Tie Fighter without Challenge Points

Pause the game, and then hold Left on the D-pad and hold C-Left + C-Down + C-Right + L Shift + R Shift + Z. While holding these buttons, you can press Up or Down on the joystick to change into the different starships.

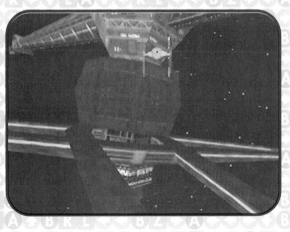

A
B
C
D
E
F
G
H
I
J
K
L
M
N
O
P
Q
R
S
T
U
V
W
X
Y
Z

Wampa Sound Effects

Enter your name as R_Testers_ROCK.

Debug Menu

This menu gives you access to the following cheats:

> **Get all stuff**
>
> **Invincibility**
>
> **50 lives**
>
> **Sleeping villains**
>
> **Kill Dash**
>
> **Teleport**
>
> **Jump to the last, the present, or the next level**
>
> **Walk through walls**

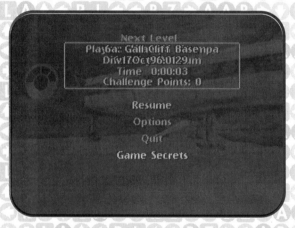

1. **Enter your name as _Wampa__Stompa. (Remember: There is one space before Wampa and two spaces between Wampa and Stompa.) Both words are case-sensitive.**

2. **Begin any level, and pause the game.**

3. **Hold down all C buttons + Z + L Shift + R Shift + Left on the D-pad.**

4. **While still holding all of these down, push the joystick halfway to the left, and hold it until you hear a sound (you will need to hold it for about five seconds). Then do the same thing, however, this time to the right. Repeat this process again to the left, back to the right, and then finally again to the left.**

5. **Text should appear at the top of the screen. Use L Shift and R Shift to change options. Push the joystick Up or Down to change some of the options. Press A to activate a code.**

6. To access the Cheat Menu again, simply pause the game, hold down all the buttons used in Step 3 and move the joystick Left or Right.

GameShark Codes

EFFECT	CODE
Unlimited lives	800E05Cb00FF
Unlimited missiles	800E126500FF

SUPER MARIO 64

Game Shark Codes

EFFECT	CODE
Half Mario	8033B2210000
Level select	A032D58C0001
Limbo Mario	8033B3B3C00C0
Mario runs backwards	8033B3bE0080
Monsters don't hurt Mario	A125460EFFFF
Monsters don't hurt Mario	A125460C240B
Monsters don't hurt Mario	A1254610A54B
Monsters don't hurt Mario	A12546120026
Monsters don't hurt Mario	A12546141000
Monsters don't hurt Mario	A1254616000C
Press GS button for 99 Coins	8933B2180063
Remove Mario's cap	A1254A300000
Remove Mario's cap	A1254A320000

EFFECT	CODE
Unlimited energy/breath	8133B21E08FF
Unlimited lives	8033B21D0064
Walk up hills	A1253DAC000
Walk up hills	A1253DAE000
Walk up hills	A1253DB0000
Walk up hills	A1253DB2000

TETRISPHERE

Special Characters

Press L Shift + C-Right + C-Down to go between numbers and special characters at the Enter Name screen.

Credits

Enter CREDITS as your name.

Hidden Game

Enter LINES as your name. Remove a large enough area at the core to free your friend.

Hidden Tunes

Enter G(alien head)MEBOY as your name. Go to Audio in the Options or pause the game.

Level Select

Enter (saturn) (spaceship) (rocket) (heart) (skull) as your name.

Extra Robot Animation

Enter VORTEX as your name, then press and hold the Reset button on the N64. After four seconds, it will show an animation with all the robots getting sucked into a vortex and then loops until the Reset button is released.

GameShark Code

EFFECT	CODE
Infinite Misses	80112F9F0003

TOP GEAR RALLY

Alternate Colors

To change the color of your car without going into the Paint Shop, highlight the car you want to use. Then hold L Shift + R Shift + C-Up + C-Down + C-Left + C-Right and press Up or Down. Pressing Up changes the color to white and pressing Down changes it to black. Hold L Shift + R Shift + C-Left or C-Up or C-Right to change to another color.

Bonus Tracks

Place first on each track during the sixth season to gain access to the Strip Mine. Place first on each track during the sixth season of the second year to gain access to the Mirror Strip Mine.

Access All Tracks

Select Arcade Mode and press A, Left, Left, Right, Down, Z. Note that this will *not* give you the mirror tracks.

Access All Cars

Select Arcade Mode and press A, Left, Left, C-Down, A, Right, Z. This code will only give you the 9 regular cars.

Bonus Cars

After defeating each season you will earn new cars as follows.

Second Season

Type-CE (Toyota Celica)
Type-IP (Isuzu P)

Third Season
Type-M3 (BMW M3)
Type-SP (Toyota Supra)

Fourth Season
Type-NS (Nissan GTIR)
Type-RS (Ford RS 200)

Fifth Season
Type-PS (Porsche)

Mirror Season (Final Season)
Milk Truck

Helmet Car
Defeat the Second Year.

Cupra Car (Ice Cube)
Defeat the Third Year.

Beach Ball Car
Defeat the Fourth Year.

Mirror Cars
Defeat the Sixth Year. As you select your car press C-Down to toggle between mirror and normal.

Completion Date
At the Title screen, hold down all four C buttons to get the completion date of the game.

Rainbow Mode

During gameplay, press C-Down, Z, B, Up, Up, Right.

Rough Edges

During gameplay, press B, Left, Right, Up, Left, Z, Right.

Credits Cheat

Go to the Credits icon in the Options menu, and press Left, C-Down, Right, Down, Z.

> EXTRA SPECIAL THANKS TO:
> MOM & DAD,
> DOLLY, MERRILL, VAL, LIZ, TIKI
> ENYA, MARVIN, # HOTTUB,
> WHITE BOMBERMAN,
> THE LOVELY CLARE,
> THE MONITOR LIZARD
> WOT BIT ROB,
> MISTRESS NICOLLE,

GameShark Codes

EFFECT	CODE
Extra Vehicles	803243CC00FF
Extra Vehicles	803243CD00FF
Level 1 Points	8032431F0064
Level 2 Points	803243210064
Level 3 Points	803243230064
Level 4 Points	803243250064
Level 5 Points	803243270064
Level 6 Points	803243290064
Extra Tracks	803243CE00FF
Extra Tracks	803243CF00FF

TUROK DINOSAUR HUNTER

GameShark Codes

EFFECT	CODE
Activate Pulse Rifle	80128E570001
Activate Quad Rocket Launcher	80128E670001
Activate Alien Weapon	80128E6B0001
Activate Chronoscepter	80128E730001
Activate Fusion Cannon	80128E6F0001
Activate Mini Gun	80128E5B0001
Activate Particle Accelerator	80128E630001
Unlimited Rifle/ Alien/Particle Ammo	80128E0B00FF

EFFECT	CODE
Unlimited Chronoscepter Ammo	80128E3300FF
Unlimited Fusion Cannon Ammo	80128E2F00FF
Unlimited Mini Gun Ammo/ Unlimited Quad	80128E2300FF
Rocket Ammo	80128E2B00FF
Unlimited Tek Arrows	80128E0F00FF
Activate Assault Rifle	80128E530001
Activate Automatic Shotgun	80128E4f0001
Activate Grenade Launcher	80128E5f0001
Activate Pistol	80128E470001
Activate Shotgun	80128E4B0001
All Keys	80128E830007
	80128E870007
	80128E8b0007
	80128E8f0007
	80128E930007
	80128E970007
	80128E9B0007

WAR GODS

GameShark Codes

EFFECT	CODE
Unlimited time	8033F31B0063

WAVE RACE

GameShark Codes

EFFECT	CODE
Only play Glacier Coast	800DA7530007
Infinite time Stunt Mode	801C295E00ff
Super speed	801C27C70050
Maximum power	801C27C70005
Right shoulder turbo boost	801C27C70005
	D01540510010
	801C27C70020
99 Points	801CB0A30063
Infinite "Course Out" time	801C298300FF
Misses don't count	801C27CF0000
Maximum power (Player 2)	801C2DEA0005

WAYNE GRETZKY'S 3D HOCKEY '98

Old Teams

At the Options screen, hold L Shift while pressing C-Right, C-Left, C-Left, C-Right, C-Left, C-Left, C-Right, C-Left, C-Left. This gives you access to Hartford, Minnesota, Quebec, and Winnipeg.

Choose Your Opponent

Highlight the team you want to play against, and then press C-Right three times. When entered correctly, you'll hear a click sound.

Debug Mode

At the Options screen, press C-Down + R Shift, C-Left + R Shift or C-Up + R Shift.

When done correctly, a window appears at the bottom of the screen that enables you to modify a 16-bit register.

You can only change the first 6 bits. To alter the bits, use the following controls:

C-Down + R Shift:	Changes head size
C-Left + R Shift:	Changes body size
C-Up + R Shift:	Changes height

The following are a few of the cooler combinations:

100000:	Stocky Players
010000:	Stocky Players, Big Heads
110000:	Stocky Players, Small Heads
001000:	Small Players, Small Announcer
000100:	Large Players, Large Announcer
000010:	Crunched Players, Small Announcer
000001:	Elongated Players, Large Announcer
110110:	Large Players, Small Heads, Large Announcer
010010:	Crunched Players, Large Heads, Small Announcer
010101:	Large Players, Large Heads, Large Announcer
010001:	Elongated Players, Large Heads, Large Announcer

Advertisements

Anytime outside of gameplay, press the Z trigger repeatedly to view the advertisements.

More Fighting

At the Options screen, highlight Fighting and hold L Shift and press C-Right, C-Left, C-Left, C-Right, C-Down, C-Up, C-Up, C-Down, C-Left, C-Right, C-Right, C-Left, C-Right, C-Left.

End Game

Pause the game and at the Options screen, hold L Shift and press C-Left (X9). This should end the game when you return.

GameShark Codes

EFFECT	CODE
Team 1 scores 50 points	8011c0610032
Team 2 scores 50 points	8011f5710032
Team 1 scores 0 points	8011c0610000
Team 2 scores 0 points	8011f5710000

WCW VS NWO

Play as Diamond Dallas Page

Defeat the WCW League Challenge to add Diamond Dallas Page to the WCW roster.

Diamond Dallas Page

Play as Randy Savage

Defeat the NWO League challenge to add Randy Savage to the NWO roster.

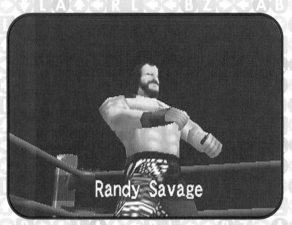

Randy Savage

Play as Glacier

Defeat the DOA league challenge to add Glacier to the DOA roster.

Play as Wrath

Defeat the IU League challenge to add Wrath to the IU roster.

WWW League

Win all four Heavyweight challenges to reveal the **WWW League** Heavyweight challenge. Win both CruiserWeight challenges to reveal the **WWW League** CruiserWeight challenge.

Play as Joe Bruiser

Defeat the multitude of opponents in the WWW's Heavyweight challenge to access this brutal boxer.

Joe Bruiser

Black Widow

Defeat everyone on the WWW's CruiserWeight challenge to access this tough female wrestler.

BlackWidow

GameShark Codes

EFFECT	CODE
Player 1 Has Aluminum Bat	810F1C200000 800F1C220000 800F080A0064
Player 1 Has Baseball Bat	810F1C200101 800F1C220000 800F080A0064
Player 1 Has Chair	810F1C200202 800F1C220000 800F080A0024
Player 1 Has Table Leg	810F1C200303 800F1C220000 800F080A0024
Player 2 Has Aluminum Baseball Bat	810F1C400000 800F1C420001 800F0BAA0064
Player 2 Has Baseball Bat	810F1C400101 800F1C420001 800F0BAA0064
Player 2 Has Chair	810F1C400202 800F1C420001 800F0BAA0024
Player 2 Has Table Leg	810F1C400303 800F1C420001 800F0BAA0024

EFFECT	CODE
Player 3 Has Aluminum Baseball Bat	810F1C600000
	800F1C620002
	800F0F4A0064
Player 3 Has Baseball Bat	810F1C600101
	800F1C620002
	800F0F4A0064
Player 3 Has Chair	810F1C600202
	800F1C620002
	800F0F4A0024
Player 3 Has Table Leg	810F1C600303
	800F1C620002
	800F0F4A0024
Player 4 Has Aluminum Baseball Bat	810F1C800000
	800F1C820003
	800F12EA0064
Player 4 Has Baseball Bat	810F1C800101
	800F1C820003
	800F12EA0064
Player 4 Has Chair	810F1C800202
	800F1C820003
	800F12EA0024
Player 4 Has Table Leg	810F1C800303
	800F1C820003
	800F12EA0024
Extra Characters	8006066500FF
Infinite Time	800F16EF0000
Maximum Spirit Player 1	800F08010064
Maximum Spirit Player 2	800F0BA10064
No Spirit Player 1	800F08010000
No Spirit Player 2	800F0BA10000

WHEEL OF FORTUNE

GameShark Codes

EFFECT	CODE
Extra Cash, Player 1	810B9992FFFF

YOSHI'S STORY

GameShark Codes

These codes require a N64 Keycode GameShark.

EFFECT	CODE
Must be on	DE0004000000
Sound always off	801DCB9E0001